The Miriam Poems

Eleanor Wolfe Hoomes

Vabella Publishing
P.O. Box 1052
Carrollton, Georgia 30112
www.vabella.com

Manufactured in the United States of America

13-digit ISBN   978-1-957479-65-1

10 9 8 7 6 5 4 3 2 1

For Miriam,
who exists only in my imagination

TABLE OF CONTENTS

LIKE A LYRIC POEM

In the beginning
life is a lyric poem.

With the onset of memory and
awareness of self in time and place,
the self plunges into narrative
through filtered recall.

In a life of consciousness,
the self exists as
both object
and observing subject,

activated by hunger, love,
hate, envy, desire,
empowered by imagination,
moderated by reason,

creating fairy tales
of spiraling linearity.
A lyric poem is an idea
rooted in the moment, non-linear.

A narrative demands mutability.
A lyric poem is immutable,
eternally true, perfect,
can exist outside time forever.

As the last arc is lived,
narrative spirals into lyric.

1

FAITH

According to my parents and their church,
with its strict religious doctrines,
requiring adherence to rigid dictates and rites,
if I only believed, had faith, and followed
the strictures, my soul would be safe for all eternity.

It seemed so simple- follow the rules and perform
the rites without deviation. Do this. Don't do that.
Do not cut my hair. Since my god was a paternal god,
he would punish me if I cut the glory of my hair.
He might even withdraw his promise of life eternal.

Do not wear men's clothing, speak in church.
Do believe and pray. God existed because I believed.
How little it took to satisfy a developing mind.
My parents were harsh in their desires to make sure
I would be taken up in the Rapture.

I believed my soul was assured eternal existence,
a heavenly promise I trusted until world religions,
mythologies, philosophies, science, reason, and
contradictions began seeping in, raising questions
the church answered with, "Have faith."

Then doubts and more doubts crept in,
followed by searches for alternatives
promising some form of continual existence.
Sans church and family, I could not yet forego
the seduction of the promise of eternal life.

BETRAYAL

The betrayal left
me feeling as
though all the
bones in my
body were smashed.

Time tells me
they have mended,
but I still
can not walk.
I do not

remember how to
stand, put one
foot in front
of the other.
Faltor, step, stride.

It has been
too long between
the strike of
lightning and the
promise of thunder.

WHY I KEEP A JOURNAL

Keeping a journal deepens my life,
anchors it, frames events and thoughts,
juxtaposes each by the other.
Eventually all organize themselves,
fold into supported meanings,
leaning against each other,
propping each other up,
clarifying, enriching.

THE SELF

Leased by humans for brief interludes,
the self is bigger than itself,
yet it is subordinate, indebted
to the unity of its fragments, attempting
to plug the loopholes of wholeness–
no matter– each self has an arc all its own.

Acting in an unscripted reality drama,
sans its producers and directors,
broken across with slashes of insight,
the self packs everything needed
for an eternity of light traveling
on the mobius strip of twisting infinity.

WHERE I DWELL

The present is where I dwell
while awaiting the future
that will never happen the way
I visualize it.
I need the imagined future
to replace the lived-in past,
a house, almost forgotten
but vaguely familiar, I sold
for a pittance years ago.

Time relocates me into abodes
nowhere, close to somewhere,
where candles glow
but do not illuminate,
where I try to solve the riddle
of home, trying to figure out
what and why I am
and am not and
where and how I want to live.

My present straddles a divide
between yesterday and tomorrow,
the beginning and the end.
I strive to adapt my life from
a universal every-woman plot
into an original story,
reflecting
ever present complexity
and never absent ambiguity.

MUSEUM

I look at the art with awed eyes.
I see just a bit of the vast diversity
concentrated in rectangles and squares.
I gaze in wonder upon the mystery
of the ordinary made extraordinary,
complexities upon complexities
of human existence, experience,
at anguished eyes, begging hands,
human ugliness made beautiful by art
transcending human flesh.

Art winks at Time and Mystery.
The angular modern, the golden ancient,
seemingly overt, yet sub rosa,
full of some other meaning
than the one I see glowing on the canvases
surrounding, embracing, infusing me.
I aspire to solve the square root of truth,
to delve deep into enlightenment,
yet I know I fail to grasp the full magnitude
of the artist's passions.

IN THE FUTURE

Written history
with its dog-eared emphasis
on white men and wars
and its hard straight edges
will be replaced–
not by warrior princesses and Amazons–
but by soft, rounded, nurturing curves.

First I will dance for myself
and then for others
as the desire to amass and surround
myself with the material trappings
of the American dream
decreases,
vanishes.

When, as an elder, I choose to die,
a golden glow will surround me
as I break free from gravity
then launch into the solved mystery of death,
where I'll drift as long as I please
in the maze of space–
now scrutable and safe.

OR

Or,
it might be
that the human life span
is all I'll have–
that death is not a comma
but a period,
signifying an inscrutable conclusion.
Perhaps "The Book of Life"
concludes with "The End."
Then slams shut for eternity.

THIS IS THE MOMENT

This is the moment when I see again
the red berries of Chinese hollies and heavenly bamboo,
trees undressing, summer failing, and in the open sky,
migrations of hummingbirds. I close the photo album,
a return ticket to once upon a time.

Shadows form, vague shapes flicker.
My thoughts begin to think themselves, prod
at the soft edges of facts, probing for an entrance.
Love doesn't disappear when it's supposed to leave;
it doesn't shimmy away because of a signed document.

I scroll back to a time before I signed the papers
meant to prove I didn't love him any more,
back to a time when I measured my life by his kisses,
before I slept alone, when I thought I was happy,
back to a time before I knew I wasn't.

I imagine and reimagine alternative scenarios.
Maybe I should have given it more time,
kept on forgiving. Maybe I could have
continued our story from the point I ended it,
reignited his love with the fire of my rekindled passion.

Maybe.
I create more scenarios of a continuing love story.
My life has been held together by stories,
but there's this gap between the story it was
and the story I wanted it to be.

Truth intrudes into my whitewash of history.
I flounder on the fact of our destructive incompatibility,
a reminder that if too much of the past
nudges itself into the present,
the future changes.

It is time to banish the Ghost of Marriage Past.
Maybe vanishes into the mists of once upon a time,
without the consolation of happily ever after.

LOST GARDEN

A garden at its most beautiful
opens a deep ache of desolation,
stirs a memory,
a longing for a never forgotten Eden
without original sin.

A familiar scent, an echo from the past,
returns me to the Lost Garden
where I looked toward the future
with anticipation and dread.
I absorbed the myths, the legendary lies,

before I could understand the
restrictions of my wonderworld.
A deep internal compass eternally
points me toward the Lost Garden,
where I knew less and less

but wanted more and more.
I longed for latitudes and longitudes
forbidden in my Paradise.
I mourn what was lost,
yet never wish to return to the time

before my world dissolved,
before enduring the possibilities
of the looming evenings,
never rue the price I paid
for independence– permanent exile.

FROM MIRIAM'S JOURNAL

"One's destination is never a place
but a new way of looking at things." Henry Miller

For me, there are two kinds of time-
the now, this moment, and the
overarching gestalt time
of past and future.

Memory leaves and returns,
never downsizes,
never recognizes redundancy
nor how to depress the delete key.

I go to bed each night with hope
clutched tight in my heart and
with a Glock 19 loaded with memories
tucked under my pillow.

I want an opening, an aperture,
an opportunity to merge with something
larger than myself.   Willing to explore,
I follow too many false leads.

The challenge of exploration propels me
from the life I've known how to live
into a space where I've been forced
to reinvent myself each day.

I need to gather the courage
to say yes or even no. There is no one
waiting on the other edge of the abyss,
holding out a helping hand.
With eyes wide open,
I'll have to leap on my own.

It is one of life's many paradoxes
that anything that takes me out of myself
also restores me to myself
with more understanding.
Passionate interests have a truth-needle
that keeps me grounded, focused.

I am coming to agree with Basho,
"Every day is a journey,
and the journey itself is home."

Yet, like T.S. Eliot, I continue
"...wavering between the profit and loss,
in the brief transit where the dreams cross."

THE NEXT SONATA

I stroll through air embracing me
like a warm bath, air I could drown in.
Beethoven's "Moonlight Sonata"
seeps from an open window,

entices me down a shadowed path.
I open a screen door, cross the porch,
knock, wait on the welcome mat.
The house is now mute, locked in sleep.

The door creaks open a crack;
a sliver of light illuminates my standing
on the welcome mat with outstretched hands,
then slams shut, is dead bolted.

Once my life moved in loose coils,
and I thrived in intertwined circles,
but I worked my way outward,
upward, each choice winnowing

relationships, jettisoning friends,
barricading dependence. The screen
door slaps in the breeze as I trudge
toward the next sonata only I can hear.

I TRY TO LISTEN

I try to listen,
sit still, be quiet.
There's something I need to hear.
Maybe if my grasp were greater,
a chorus of existence might sing to me,
but meaning is a fellow traveler,
running alongside me, unseen, unheard.

Messages are rained, blown,
hummed in nonwords
at frequencies I strain to hear.
I seek answers to a question
which must be reinvented with each asking.
Nonverbal responses
just beyond my reach elude me.

Perhaps I can travel the universe
by holding still,
linger at crossroads,
ignore the beckoning spokes,
no choices necessary.

ONE DAY SOON

The rain wails,
holds me captive in its musty privacy,
bathes me in the intimacy of fatigue.
The torrents gush through gutters,
overflow drains, followed
by the monotonous drip, drip, drip
of droplets plopping from leaves and eaves,
sliding down windowpanes, reminding
me I exist alone in a country of rain.

I escape from my dank, dark dungeon
to slosh among the trees restraining the storm,
their canopy propping up the darkness.
Washed clean air erases my lethargy.
I knock on trunks, listens for a twanging note,
a splashing plink, a secret, anything.
The landscape remains soaked in silence.

Drenched to the bone, shivering,
I return to my yellow-lit kitchen
now bright with pots of basil and rosemary,
a banked fire, split pea soup simmering.
I pick up the travel book tossed face down,
study the map spread across the table
promising–

Life bursts from a rain-barred cell,
streaks toward the horizon
in search of the primitive language of a promise,
the heat of possibility that can fast-beat a heart
too long alone in a country of rain.

One day soon–

ABSTRACT

A glimmer of an idea, transmutes
into a vision suggesting organic themes,
subjectively reducing reality
with deconstructed forms
obscuring details–
purity synthesized with composition and mass.
Line, the protagonist, creates a rhythmic series,
decisive, definite,
unified with color,
molded with brushes, spatulas, bristles, blades–
inspiration, execution.

An amalgam of disunifying themes,
deconstructed dissonance,
assaults me.
Disconnected from figurative references,
rebelling against the tyranny of tradition,
color unifies form, line, structure,
obscures the external, obscures reality,
changes, expands, transforms.
For a brief moment I believe
my imagination has translated, captured,
absorbed the essence of truth.

Yet truth might exist farther than I can see,
might be more than I can bear.

VICTORY

The anticipated annual
emergence of Persephone
ushering in another spring–
days sunnier, longer.

I am one day richer,
basking in the sun's light.
From Morpheus's arms,
I wake early, welcome

Helios rising over
the horizon of the lake,
piloting his golden
chariot from East to

West, waking, warming,
scattering a wisp of
cloud, each day taking
longer and longer victory

laps. I stretch, bow to the
East, to Persephone for
her lavish gift of greens,
silvers, roses, purples,

and to golden Helios
gilding my day, my life.

FIRST DAY

First Day– a crazy quilt
blanket-stitched together with primroses,
tea olives, daphnes, daffodils, jonquils–
exploding with the joy of being alive.

A blustery day of scudding clouds
in a sky so blue if captured on canvas,
would look fake– I fly free,
darting among the white-capped clouds.

I embrace every whiff of fresh air,
each breath the intoxicating stuff
I use to create new universes
in my fantasies.

Mother Nature parades in her finery
on this first day– she struts–
removes her bonnet so she and I
can bask in the sun's kinetic rays.

She presents me with the miracle
that keeps me alive, feeling as if
she has me on her speed dial, as if
what she spreads before me is all mine.

Words, images flick through my mind–
exquisite, elation, roses roving wild–
She assists me in yanking out the last
remnants of winter darkness.

"Please stay," I plead. "Please stay.
Help me plant deep the joys of today."

JUST OUT OF REACH

It would be accommodating,
just plain good manners,
if that male cardinal perched on the cedar snag
at the edge of my back yard flew closer
to my porch rocker. I'd like to observe him up close–

his red crest, the full black "beard"
surrounding his orange-red beak,
his eyes, the details of his wings, his feet,
the layering of his vibrant crimson feathers,
the way the sun sets those scarlet feathers aflame.

I could watch the three squirrels playing tag
in the dog's kennel. The dog is sprawled
in her damp sandbox, cooling her hot self.
White dog, brown squirrels– so tame, so available–
can't compete with flying vermillion.

The cardinal calls, "So sweet, so sweet, so sweet,
see here, see here, see here, tup, tup, tup."
I want him to fly closer; only he will suffice.
But he does not; instead, he cocks his head,
teasing me, "So sweet, so sweet, so sweet,"

just out of reach– like so much in life.

VANQUISH THE DARK

At the end of the year, along with other rituals
of Celtic, pagan, and Christian origins,
I decorate my home with Christmas ferns,
plants that do not go dormant nor die
during winter– symbols of immortality.

After the longest night of Winter Solstice,
Earth tilts toward the light.
At the crux, I feel the pith of life,
hope for truths to be made clearer.
I fling a plea to the universe,

"Make my days longer; baptize me in light;
help me vanquish the dark
and make manageable each night.
Help me live like my Christmas ferns–
strong enough to survive, flourish, thrive."

TAIL WINDS

The sonance of an airplane assaults
the shepherd's satellite ears. She points,
then sits, looks up, wuffs, ears rotating
to capture the diminishing vibrations.

I track the lights of the plane.
It is pleasant to imagine the passengers
having a good time, flushed with anticipation,
already a little tipsy, gamblers abandoning

mundane lives, nurturing the need
to be some place else, to encounter strange
cultures with wonder and dread, where
foreign beliefs thrum through their heads

as they fight secret prejudices running deeper
than underground rivers– deformed biases
encouraging the animal parts of themselves
to fear, to hate what they don't understand.

Something stronger than yearning sizzles
in my veins, sharp, quick, agile, rhythmic,
dancing rumbas and jitterbugs,
eager to boogie across the skyscape.

Big Bang, evolution,
mythology, Zodiac,
western civilization,
heaven–

Tired of knowing nothing, I am willing
to gamble on tail winds and soothsayers,
ready to trade the wreck of the past
with its dark shadows smothering the present

for the freedom to soar through the future.
The white shepherd yelps, pats me with a paw,
leaps circles around me, ears laid flat,
and herds me back home

JOY

Dream and reality overlap, fuse, anneal.
Pine and honeysuckle scent the heavy air.
The water is Coca-Cola-bottle green,
clear to the bottom where fissured light
ripples across the sand.
I read or heard the broken patterns of light
reflected on the bay bottom are the same
as the designs on a giraffe's back and
the same as the cracks in dried red clay.

The water reflects the sun, yet underneath
mirrors trees, vines, sand, rocks,
and my own image.
Like Narcissus, I gaze at myself,
but not in admiration. I'm striving to fathom
the eternal and elemental mysteries
surrounding me, and to internalize
the ephemeral joy suffusing me.
Dreams and reality overlap, fuse, anneal.

TO KNOW OR NOT TO KNOW

I stroll the beach, late evening ebb tide
lapping at my bare feet
after dissolving abandoned sand castles.
I am striving to remember my deceased mother,
whom I had not seen in decades before her death.
I cannot evoke her face, her smile,
her touch, her laugh.
Even now I do not know why
I grew up without a mother's love.
No one is alive who can enlighten me.

Much was hidden, much submerged.
I am left to gather artifacts washed up like rubble
on the shores of the present,
uneasy about the undiscovered treasures
now lying within reach.
Ghostly fragments tantalize with glimpses,
flashbacks too vague to latch onto.
I touch the letter in my pocket,
mailed to me by my late father's lawyer.
Maybe it will satisfy my need to know.

Should I open and read the letter, or
do I set it afloat, unopened, on the ebbing tide?
To know or not to know–
I sit on a sand dune, undecided,
then tear open the letter.
The truth isn't always what one wishes it to be.
It isn't always small enough to absorb at once.
Sometimes truth does not set one free.
Sometimes the truth swamps one
and threatens to wash one out to sea.

Later I regret I had not set the letter,
unopened, adrift on the ebbing tide.

ENTANGLED

I am entangled by my past, trapped
in a cocoon of regret, blaming others.
Should haves and should not haves
cling to and choke my soul,
keeping my life stalled on hold.
I must find the strength within myself
to slash the web to shreds,
emerge like a butterfly
to soar untethered and free.

STILL IN SHADOWS

Green mold flourishes, envelops the surface
of the moon–encroaching nocturnal darkness.
An amorphous blob of dread evolves
into a chimera, a fire-breathing monster, twitching
its serpent's tail in shadows, eager to pounce.

I rend the rind, tearing at it, breaking nails,
flaying it off the moon in strips, implore
the sun's rays to bounce from craters and dust,
to reflect again the energy of the sun,
diluted for nighttime consumption.

Still in shadows,
entrenched amorphous dread lurks,
impatient,
eager
for green mold to regrow.

IMAGES

Stereoscopic images,
merge, intermingle, crowd my head–

Click!
A View-Master rearranges shapes, colors, scenes.
I stroll arm in arm with an ex-lover at sunset.
I lean into the scene to capture its essence,
reexperience our expressions, gestures, whispers.

Click!
Swans drift in swirling purple snow.
In a pink tutu, I tango atop a hybrid SUV,
pirouette down, watch and listen to
Sunday's "Karaoke for Christ" vocalize cacophony.

Click!
Flashes of a wintertime woodland glade intrude.
Echoes dance down miles of Red Carpet.
Harps sing with quivering strings.
Instruments blend into a symphony.

Click!
An empowered woman, I run with wolves,
eluding vipers concealed beneath beauty.
A wind ensemble parades by a bandstand,
pursed lips blowing into silver flutes.

Click!
The sun shines into my head– illuminates.
Pictures, scents, tastes, textures, sounds
collide, combine, evolve into words,
develop individual, distinct voices.

Click!
The images will be voiced, understood. Just so.
I pay a single peppercorn to the images,
plead with them to remain domiciled rent free
in my imagination in perpetuity.

Stereoscopic images merge, intermingle
crowd my head, produce poetry.

BEWILDERED

What will I become in the next hour?
Bewildered, under neon,
I hold a furled umbrella,
tote full of books offering no answers.

In a constant state of inexactitude—
the plans for my life had been specific—
if I speak to someone,
it's just to leave things out.

Armored against a greedy world,
asking and taking,
accoutered against the bottom
of the beckoning river,

I trudge past welcoming cafes,
all-night eateries.
Hungry not for food;
no longer hungry for empty words.

But hungry, nonetheless.
The book tote bumps against my hip.
If only I could believe in something,
anything, again with certitude.

I fling the books into the river,
one by one.

PRIME REALITY

Another spring seduces with promises of immortality.
Emerging greens, traitors to a recently deceased winter,
fill begging bowls with jewels of regeneration.
The blood of the surviving flows smoother, less erratic.
The sun propagates new freckles, burnishes old.
Petals spiral from the sky, fall singed at my feet.

The sun thumbs through the Book of Light while
ungrieved winter becomes a fading dark memory,
and the past reclaims its own.
The breeze blows swift through graying hair
as I sit on warmed rocks, drinking in cloudless skies,
and shatter into a thousand happy pieces.

Then– I am slapped with prime reality–
another year has come and gone. Old age creeps
on silent feline feet, discriminating against the Self,
and I am a year closer to somewhere I'll go alone.
Yet, birds sing soprano above the sounds of spring,
and my thousand happy pieces bask in a honey glow.

Perhaps for a moment, time will pause, vanish,
and then striped bare, without the stain
of my shadow, I may stare at my true self.

TOWARD THE END

Some people want the world.
I just want to inhabit my own corner
where advancing age can creep in unnoticed,
and I can slip out unmourned when time
has seeped through the cracks of immortality
and punctured my complacency.

For too long, I have been living with the
psychological inconvenience of indecision and guilt
without the consolation of certainty or absolution
offered by a deceased and interred God.
I sleep little at night, nod off often during the day,
bedeviled by dreams of that long-buried God.

Yet, my heart is as full of fire and ice
as when I first met love. How odd
to think now how sex had been so simple
and love such a complication.
Did I give up too soon on that first love?
Did I jettison too easily my love for God?

NOT MY HOME

Nothing much has changed
in the sheltered chambers of my heart,
but the susceptible corners
of my mind are increasingly shrouded.

A flash, a glimmer
triggers memories–
life is still miraculous–
a smell, a touch
a poem, ah poetry–
a half forgotten line from a song,
"This world is not my home,
I'm only passing through...."

I peer through obscuring scrims
attempting to unveil images,
prize apart brittle glue
searching for words.
Even the poetry is fading–
fading–
"And I can't feel at home
in this world anymore...."

SENIOR MOMENTS

Senior moments sneak into my life,
create situations for what I value
and rely on to break free, plummet,
land upside down and turn inside out.

Things my elders, books, art, life taught me
and my sense of humor steal away in the dark
of night, their absence seldom missed
in the light of a new day.

My brain sheds old cells, does not create new.
Once obedient thought processes rebel.
Long held beliefs, ground rules, rites vanish
as nouns lose their names, verbs their actions.

I always took my brain for granted,
thought it would never change,
but here I am striving to right myself
in altered currents of brain waves.

I am trying to learn to live
in the life of the stranger
I'm becoming, unrelieved
by laughter's brief amnesia.

MIRIAM'S FRIEND

I sit with my friend, Miriam,
who carved her life out of dream stone.
Her mind is almost exiled from her body.
My friend is farther away from herself
than we are from each other,
sitting on opposite ends of a park bench,
waiting for we know not what.
At the last moment as the sun sets,
Miriam looks at me,
lost to our world, puzzled.
"Now, just who am I?" she asks.
And then–
"I don't know how to get home."

ACKNOWLEDGEMENTS

I wish to thank the following people:

My editor and technical advisor, Angelia Hoomes;
Angelia Hoomes, Ben Jordan, and Charlsie Sprewell for the
cover of THE MIRIAM POEMS;
Dr. Bob Covel for making suggestions and corrections;
PenPal members Claire Baker, Beverly Bruemmer, Cecilia
Lee, and Donna Spivey for their suggestions and support;
Members of Just Poetry for their valuable insights;
John Bell, my patient publisher, and
the readers of my previous volumes of poetry for their
encouragement.

Eleanor Wolfe Hoomes   July 2023

Made in the USA
Columbia, SC
25 September 2023

23216760R00029